I0479600

How To Start a Business

How To Start a Business

AKA Who Stole My Pigs?
A Beginner's Guide To Starting A Business

Roger M. Rowan

Copyright © 2022 by Roger M. Rowan.

ISBN:	Softcover	978-1-6698-3812-8
	eBook	978-1-6698-3811-1

All rights reserved. No part of this book may be reproduced or transmitted in any form or by any means, electronic or mechanical, including photocopying, recording, or by any information storage and retrieval system, without permission in writing from the copyright owner.

Any people depicted in stock imagery provided by Getty Images are models, and such images are being used for illustrative purposes only.
Certain stock imagery © Getty Images.

Print information available on the last page.

Rev. date: 07/20/2022

To order additional copies of this book, contact:
Xlibris
844-714-8691
www.Xlibris.com
Orders@Xlibris.com
843553

To my mother and father who gave me my start in business
and also funded part of my college education.

Advice from an entrepreneur
with tips and ideas
you may need to know
if you want to start a business.

Acknowledgment

I would also like to thank Bruce Dana who spent many hours proofreading my material.

Thank you.

Contents

How to Start a Business

Who Stole My Pigs?

Roger M. Rowan

You're in Business

So you want to start a business. Congratulations. That's fantastic! Good luck. Starting a business is not that hard. Just offer a product or service that you can do and *bam*—you're in business. The objective, however, is to make money out of it. Sometimes, the business may only last one day, and you make your money all in "one shot." But most of the time, you want to maintain that business and make it last for a long time. For example, let's say you buy an apple and turn around and sell it for more than what you paid for it. You're in business. You made a profit. If you continue to buy apples and sell them for more than what you paid for them, at some point, you may be able to switch over and buy a PC. (Sorry for the pun.)

Entrepreneur

What is an entrepreneur? People who start a business venture are called entrepreneurs. By definition, an entrepreneur is a person who makes money by starting or running a business, especially when this involves taking financial risks. (See *Oxford Learner's Dictionaries API.*)

The thesaurus says that venture means "an undertaking, scheme, project, endeavor, gamble, risk, speculation, hazard, dare, try, and embark on." I will talk more about these in the following chapters.

How Do You Know If You Are an Entrepreneur?

Many people are entrepreneurs. You may be an entrepreneur and not know it. Some people are born an entrepreneur, and some people are made one. Does it matter whether you were born or made an entrepreneur? No, I do not think so. But let's find out how you became an entrepreneur. When you were a kid, did you ever start a business or even want to start a business, like a lemonade stand? Were you known in your family as a "wheeler-dealer?" Were you always making a trade with someone for something, then trading that for something else for something better? Then you may have been a "born entrepreneur."

Or when your mother asked you to pick up your toys in the living room, did she pay you with a cookie, candy, or money if you did the job? As you got older, when your dad asked you to clean the garage, did you ask, "How much will you pay me?" Then you may have been taught to be an entrepreneur.

Here are a few more questions that might tell if you are an entrepreneur. Do you dislike getting up every morning to go to work at a certain time? Do you dislike working for a steady paycheck? Would you rather be your own boss? Would you rather start a business and then go start another one than "work" the one you just started? Are you always looking for that next "big idea"? Do you have many ideas on how to "make a million dollars"? When people see you, do they ask you, "So what is your *job du jour*?" (French for "job of the day"). And most of the time, you will have an answer that is different from the one you gave them yesterday. Then you are probably an entrepreneur.

Why Am I An Entrepreneur?

I don't know for sure why some people, including myself, have so many ideas on how to start a business, make money, or invent things, but I do have a theory. I truly believe that there are people or spirits on the other side of life that are continually coming up with these good ideas, and I think that they are putting those ideas into the astrosphere or space or subconscious for anyone to pick up on them. Some people on earth are more susceptible to these thoughts or impressions than others. I believe that some people like Galileo Galilei, Leonardo da Vinci, Albert Einstein, Orville and Wilbur Wright, Philo T. Farnsworth, Walt Disney, Bill Gates, and others just have minds who are in tune with these electrons or space particles that are floating around out there, waiting for someone to pick up and act on them. To some degree, I think I am one of those people. I don't know how to explain the fact that these ideas just come into my mind. Why do I pick up on them and others don't? I have discovered that there is usually more than one person who gets these ideas at the same time. An example would be Philo T. Farnsworth, inventor of television, who had to fight with Russian-born Vladimir Zworykin, who also thought the same idea. Mr. Farnsworth won the patent because one of his schoolteachers kept some of his early writings, and he was able to prove it in court.

There is even a name for this ability to "pick up" on ideas floating around in the air. It is called "Akashic" or "Akashic Records Independent Simultaneously Invention."

(Akashic Records Independent Simultaneously Invention. In theosophy and anthroposophy, the **Akashic records** are a compendium of all human events, thoughts, words, emotions, and intent ever to have occurred in the past, present, or future. They are believed by theosophists to be encoded in a non-physical plane of existence known as the etheric plane.)

Some people seem to have an uncanny ability to write music or books or are born with a special talent, like playing the piano or other musical instruments. I don't know why; I just know that it happens. Some people work hard and continue with the talent with which they have been born. I have a cousin, who is very talented on the piano. She was able to listen to music on the radio and pick it out on the piano at age four. I know a young boy who can read the closed captions on my television, and he has not started kindergarten. My parents use to say that when I was younger, I was always trading for something or scheming on something. I remember trading things like knives, guns, chain saws, pool tables, and other things to end up with something I wanted but then eventually trade those things too.

An example of an idea that I had but did not think was a big deal was when I invented a different way to tie a necktie. One day, I was tying a necktie around my neck. From the way I was tying it, I noticed when I was done that the inside seam of the short end of the necktie was always facing out (also see a double Windsor knot). I studied this phenomenon for a while and figured out that if I started with my tie up-side-down and made a second knot, I would end with both the front and back of the tie facing forward. I did not think any more about this until about two weeks later, on one of the daytime talk shows, the host of the show had two men on who had also figured out how to tie this same knot. Apparently, it was new and a big enough deal that they showed it on television. Where did this idea come from and how did those other people come up with it apparently about the same time I did?

Another example comes from Larry Page, who said he "*dreamt* up the idea of Google"! In 1966, college-student Larry Page feared that a clerical mistake led to his acceptance to the university. Due to this irrational fear, Page dreamt one night of downloading and storing the internet on individual computers. Soon after waking up, Page did some *simple* calculations and concluded that while it wasn't possible, he was able to create a searchable database of links to web pages. (See Larry Page.)

How an Entrepreneur Starts a Business

A bit of an overlegalization of starting a business is as follows:

Non-entrepreneur:

When starting a business, morally, a person who has not been born an entrepreneur but would like to become one will start at the beginning. He or she will study things out, observe others, make a business plan, talk to people in that business, rewrite his or her business plan, get his or her "ducks" in order, then start over by checking things out again and again, over and over. Then he or she will obtain financing, get employees trained, and strive to get everything in order before he or she starts a business. On a scale of 0 to 100, this type of person will start at 0, work to 50, and then he or she can start a business.

Entrepreneur:

On the other hand, when starting a new business, an entrepreneur may start at 50 on the same scale of 0 to 100 and go from there and find a way to make it work, or is sometimes forced to make it work. A business plan is very important, and a good entrepreneur will have one. Sometimes, it is just in his or her head. A lending institution will usually require a business plan, so the entrepreneur will have to write one. However, he or she modifies it as it goes. He or she will get financing, with or without a track record—sometimes using OPM (other people's money). He or she is impulsive, makes quick discussions, and pushes through. Entrepreneurs will hire help as they need it. In other words, they find a way to make it work. Sometimes, this works; sometimes, it does not. Sometimes, entrepreneurs are good at starting a business but not running it. They may sell the business and get out of it once it is started.

Examples

The following are some examples of things I have done, seen done, or heard of being done by entrepreneurs.

Family-Owned Businesses

Many businesses, such as store owners, restaurant owners, farmers, and other businesses get started based on the experience they have had by being around and working in a family-owned business. Fortunately, for me, this is how I got started.

As I mentioned in the beginning, I do not know when I started wheeling and dealing. It seemed to be in my blood. My dad was a farmer, but in 1959, when I was about twelve years old, my dad became friends with a businessman. He owned an insurance office and offered to teach my father how to sell insurance. My dad soon started his own insurance business in the basement of our home. Later, dad bought a small "Book of Business" from another insurance agent in a nearby town. (A "book of business" is a group of clients that an insurance business already has and then sells this business.) It grew, and soon, dad built a building and relocated his business from the basement to an office in the bigger town. Later, he earned his real estate license to go along with his insurance business. Mom worked with him as the secretary and office manager. I often went with him to see the property and became interested in his business. I saw how he listed and sold the property, as well as how he sold insurance. I wanted to work for my parents, but their business was not quite big enough to support them and me. My official training started when I started college. I decided to get a degree in business education. When I was a junior in college, I studied and obtained my real estate license and began listing and selling for him. In real estate, you have to obtain your salesmen's license, then work for a broker. After two years, you can then take a test to be a broker. I was fortunate to have a father who was already in insurance and real estate. He helped me succeed.

I remember listing a forty-acre piece of property that adjoined another farmer's land. As we visited with this man, he said he had a chance to buy that piece of land several times already but never did. He said he would like to have the property, but the price had risen, and he did not want to pay that much. In our discussion, we learned that the price of the land had steadily gone up each year. Finally, as we talked, I asked him, "Well, what do you think the price of that land is going to be tomorrow?" He bought the land. I remember my dad giving me a big compliment! He said that question about what the price would be tomorrow was what did the trick to help him buy the property. I don't know if it did or not, but the fact that my dad made me feel good about my selling ability made me feel very confident about myself.

Pay Attention to Details

I later listed an apartment complex to sell. There were about a dozen separate apartments and homes all in one deal. I put them all together and sold them to one person. One of the properties had been sold and resold before the present owners acquired it. When I was reviewing the preliminary title insurance policy, I noticed that this property had never had a deed signed or recorded. This property had been sold about eight times over. Luckily, I was able to find the original owners and had them sign a quitclaim deed to solve the problem. They were both old, and it was lucky they were still alive.

Some Is Better Than None

These properties were worth over a million dollars, and the real estate commission on these proprieties would have been very high. However, because I was selling these properties for a friend, I worked out a deal with my friend to get a flat fee for selling this property. It was not the usual real estate commission, but it was a good fee. I did the same thing with another friend who allowed me to sell a large farm. I made a flat fee again. It was good to have some commission. I have a couple of sayings that have helped me over the years. In the stock market, the old saying is "Bulls make money, bears make money, but pigs get slaughtered." In other words, "If you can't make a dollar, make fifty cents."

Experience Is a Great but Sometimes a Cruel Teacher

One of the first places you might have learned about becoming an entrepreneur and starting a business was in middle school or high school. Schools offer several business classes. You can join clubs like Future Farmers of America and 4-H. Future Farmers of America is a great place to learn the "business" of being a farmer. Many boys and girls who grew up working side by side with their parents on a farm may want to continue in the family business even after obtaining a college degree. Like most businesses, farming is a lot more technical today than it was when your grandpa farmed. Today farmers deal in large financial numbers and need to know more than the price of pork.

Speaking of the price of pork, I raised pigs as a boy. A friend of mine had access to a corral on his uncle's farm. A farmer sells baby pigs after they are about six-week-old and weigh about six to eight pounds. My friend asked me if I wanted to raise some pigs with him. We each bought twelve weaner pigs. We put his pigs on one side of the pen and mine on the other. Using my friend's pickup, we purchased feed from the feed store and gave water to them every day. We also put several old milk cans in the back of his pickup and would drive to the local cheese factory. At that time, whey was a by-product of cheese and was thrown away, but it was very healthy for pigs. We would fill several cans of whey and take them to the corrals and dump one or two cans into the trough, along with other feed, for the pigs. They loved it, it was good for them, and it really helped them gain weight. Today you can buy whey protein powder, and if you will look on the back of your favorite snack foods, you may see whey contained in them.

After raising the pigs for about six months, a pig would weigh about 180 to 220 pounds. Usually, we would make a profit of about four times the cost of the weaner pig. One day, about a week before we were going to take them to the auction to sell, I went to the corral and saw that two of my pigs had been stolen. It was wintertime, and I could see blood around the corral and a trail where they had been dragged to the road, loaded into a truck, and driven away. I was devastated. I could not believe it. I thought about reporting this to the police, but I didn't think there was anything that could be done. The people that did this would have known how to butcher the pigs themselves and would not have been so stupid as to take them to a butcher to be cut and wrapped. I sold the remaining pigs at auction and received enough money to pay all my costs, but the two that were stolen would have been my profit. We never found out who stole the pigs.

What Worked and What Didn't

What did I get from my experience as a pig farmer? Just that, experience.

Although at that time, I did not know the process of business, I did the process of business. I will be speaking about the "process" of business as we go along, but I hope by the time I get to that point, you will already know it.

What did I do right?

1. I had an idea. The idea that I could make some money.
2. I had a goal. It was to buy some weaner pigs, feed them until they were grown, and then sell them so that I could make money.
3. I was willing to take a "calculated risk."
4. I was working with experienced and knowledgeable people. Even though my friend was the same age as me, he had raised pigs before. He knew where to buy them. He knew where to keep them and what and how to feed them. He knew how to care for pigs; for example, by pouring motor oil on their backs, you can keep them from getting sunburned. He even knew how to castrate pigs. I didn't think I was getting an education as I sat on the belly of a pig, listening to it squeal at the top of its lungs, as I held the back legs apart so that my friend could play veterinarian, but I assure you, it was an education.

5. I learned that a job is an everyday thing. You have to feed and water pigs every day.
6. I learned that there is pleasurable anticipation of the success you are going to have at the end of your venture.
7. I learned to write down and keep track of expenses.
8. I learned how to economize on expenses.
9. I learned to pay my debts. I borrowed money from my dad and paid him back. I knew my dad was an experienced entrepreneur and was happy to see his kid succeed, or fail but at least try to do something new to see if he could make money. Anytime you get a child to work, you have done a good thing. I think this was the underlying motive for my dad. I learned this example well and always encouraged my own children to work when they could. Sometimes, I even created places for them to work.
10. I learned that even though you may think you are doing everything right, some things are out of your control, like when someone steals two pigs. Or when I was selling real estate and the interest rate for a home mortgage went up to 18 percent and nothing was selling.

I could have used the SMART acronym.

(In 1981, George T. Doran, a consultant for the Washington Water Power Company, published an article in the November issue of *Management Review*, created a mnemonic device for business. A mnemonic device, or memory device, is any learning technique that aids information retention or retrieval (remembering) in the human memory for better. His acronym is SMART, which stands for specific, measurable, achievable, relevant, and time-bound. Each of these tips could be very useful in setting goals to start a business.)

What did I do wrong?

1. I am not sure I can blame anything I did wrong on being young and inexperienced. If you are starting a new business

at, say, age forty, you would still be considered young for that business. There are some things that should be done at any age when starting a business. In this case, I should have been a little more skeptical about the location. I should have realized that the location was out in the open for anyone to see, and no one was watching over the pigs. I should have called the police.

2. Although I did have a good idea of what we were going to do, I did not know that I needed to write my business plan on paper. That is a must. (See business plans below.)

3. I didn't provide adequate security for my investment.

4. I knew there were people in the world who are dishonest; however, I did not know to what extent these people would go to get what they wanted. That is still extremely hard for me to grasp. (I will show another example of dishonesty below.)

If Your Banker Comes to You and Wants to Loan You Money, Do It

Speculation is something you have to be careful in doing. I am not saying you should never speculate, but there are many things that can go wrong. Here are a couple of examples of times when I speculated and made money and some wherein I lost money.

Years ago, a couple of brothers named Hunt tried to corner the market on silver. They were buying it as fast as they could. I had a thousand dollars that I had saved, so I decided to buy silver instead of leaving it in a savings account, hoping I would make more than I would from the interest from the bank. In about six or seven months, the price of silver went up, and I sold my silver and made nearly double.

As silver prices continued to go up and down, a friend of mine, who was the vice president of a bank, came to me and said he wanted to buy a bag of silver. I don't remember the exact cost, but it was too expensive for him to come up with the money by himself. He wanted me to go in with him. I told him I did not have the money to speculate with him at this time. He was very experienced in buying and selling silver and felt that this was the time to buy and said, as my banker, he would even loan me my half. I had just purchased a house and did not want to overextend myself and politely declined. Well, he went ahead and bought the silver himself and within four weeks made four times the amount of money he had invested. Here is a saying I want you to put in your head and never forget:

"IF YOUR BANKER COMES TO YOU AND WANTS TO LOAN YOU MONEY, DO IT."

A few months later, I felt that the market was in the same situation as it was when he bought his silver and went to him to see if he wanted to do it again. He felt the timing was not right this time and did not want to do it then. I asked him if he would still loan me money to buy silver. Although he thought it was the wrong time, my credit was good, and he loaned me the money. To make a long story short, the price of silver went down, and I lost ten thousand dollars. It took me a long time to pay back the loan. Moral of the story: Listen and follow the advice of people who are smarter or more experienced than you.

Failure

That brings me to another important aspect of the business, something else to look out for:

"Don't want something so much that you overlook the details."

In my example of silver, I wanted it so badly that I was willing to risk borrowing money to get it. This time involved a photography business.

I started working in the photography business when I was a student in college. I got a job in a photo store. My manager also did photography for weddings on the side. He was kind enough to teach me how to be a photographer, and within a short time, I was making money, shooting photos for a wedding and other things. Over the next thirty-five years, I supplemented my income by doing weddings, advertising, sporting events, family reunions, school pictures, and other photos. At one time, I had an opportunity to purchase a photography business. This business included a photography studio, which did film processing and printing. This was a complete photography business and included printing photos for other photographers. I really wanted this business and felt it would be a culmination of all the years of being a photographer. Several people, including my wife, advised against this, but I really wanted it. I wanted it so badly that I ignored the research I did on the value of the equipment, location, and revenue. I felt I could overcome any obstacle that stood in my way and could increase revenue by increasing the business. The seller only provided me with an older tax return from the year before and did not give me a month-to-month printout of income and expenses which, I found out later, he knew was declining. Again, I knew better and should have required more. He also failed to inform me that there was a Walmart store opening up in our community and that it would be developing and processing film at half the price that his business did. I failed to do the research on this and other businesses that processed film. When the Walmart store opened, I lost a lot of the film business immediately. In the long run, the expenses for equipment repair, employees, supplies, rent, utilities, etc., cost me way more money than I was able to generate. Needless to say, I lost this business. This was a "big learning experience." Again, never want something so badly that you ignore the facts.

Remember, if a business says they had a 200 percent increase in sales, don't be fooled into believing this is as good as it sounds. It could be that they only sold one unit last year for one dollar and sold two this year. That is a 200 percent growth, however, not in the way they may want you to think. If someone goes from one million to two million, then this may be a good growth margin.

That being said, one would not be an entrepreneur if he or she sometimes does not take risks and maybe fail.

Watch Out for Obsolete Businesses

As an entrepreneur, one will always think of things he or she can do for a business. It's all right to want it. Just be careful not to want something that will be obsolete in a short while. At one time, I thought I wanted to buy a tow truck and go into the towing business. I had a chance to buy a nice tow truck, but a friend, who was machinic, pointed out that you don't hook up to a car and tow it away anymore. Newer cars have one-piece frames. You have to carry cars on the back of tow trucks now. Towing-type trucks are obsolete. Again, do research!

Teaching at Utah State University

We each have very special times in our lives—moments that will stand out in our lives and memories forever. Some of these moments may be things like marriage, seeing children born, Christmas, graduation, and more. I have had many great memories in my life.

Two of these special times were (1) obtaining my master's degree and (2) being an adjunct professor and having the opportunity to use my degree to teach entrepreneurship and marketing at a major university. I was a public school teacher at the same time and taught my university classes at night. Being able to teach at the university level, to me, was a dream come true. My wife and daughter made it even more special by bringing donuts to me and my whole class on the first day. During those five years, I had a chance to teach in a classroom on campus and also teach a satellite class from the school that was broadcasting to about fourteen cities. One of the teaching techniques was to invite several, very successful, businesspeople into my class and have them explain what they did to start a business and how they became successful. If you follow some of the suggestions I provide for you here, you may have a greater chance of succeeding in your venture.

One of the men who spoke in my class started the biggest fireworks business west of the Mississippi River. His business did most of the fireworks for the Olympics held in Utah. He started in the kitchen of his home, where he claims he once blew off the door of his wife's stove.

Another man and his children started a towing service years ago. To gain recognition, they painted all their tow trucks and carry trucks bright orange. People who needed a tow truck would just say, "Call the guys with the orange trucks." This was a great marketing tool.

Another example was a student who had started an artesian bread company. He had hit a niche in the bread market. He was making bread and selling it to restaurants and specialty stores. He came to me and said his business was growing so big that he was going to drop my class because he had to bake his bread at night, which was the same time as my class. He wanted to know what he could do, like writing a paper, to pass the class. He was very close to the end of the class, so I said if he would bring some samples of his "bread" to class for the students, and tell them about his startup, I would pass him. He did that. He had been baking bread at night in a pizza oven after the restaurant closed for the night. Eventually, his business became so big that he had to move to a location that had an oven available to him full time. He has been making different types of bread like baguettes, sourdough, white cob, Mediterranean, grand rustic, cheese and red onion, and ciabatta bread. Some were seasoned with green and red peppers, sundried tomatoes, and even chocolate chips. The class really enjoyed his bread as he explained how he started and talked about the growth of his business. I gave him an "A."

Starting a Kool-Aid Stand

I think the most special person I had visit my class was an eleven-year-old girl. I knew this young girl's mother and got permission to have her visit my class. She was a big hit with my students. I will call her Jane. I don't think Jane knew she was the perfect entrepreneur. All she knew was she was making money. When I asked her if her business was a success, she said, "See that new twenty-one-speed bicycle over there? I paid $189 cash for it." Here is what she did to make her the perfect example of a businessperson.

In our area, grocery stores sometimes have sales on Coca-Cola and Pepsi products. I'm sure these sales are product driven as a loss leader for the stores. However, they priced a twelve-pack of Coke or Pepsi products, 7 Up, Sprite, etc., on sale for "buy three for ten or eleven dollars and get one more twelve-pack for free." This makes each can about twenty-three cents per can. Jane happened to live right next door to a post office in a small town that did not deliver mail door to door. In other words, everyone in the town had to go to the post office to get their mail. (Location, location, location.) Jane started by going to her mother and borrowing enough money to buy several twelve packs of soda. She set up a table on her mom's property, right next to the post office, put a cooler full of ice next to it, and started selling soda for fifty cents per can. She probably could have sold the soda for a dollar but found out that more people would buy the product at a lower price. However, most people would give her a dollar and tell her to keep the change. This was a glorified lemonade stand on steroids. Sometimes, when I see a lemonade stand, I stop and buy a cup because I like to encourage young entrepreneurs. But most of the time, I just drive down the street, out of sight, and pour it out. Some people, including myself, felt that because the sealed cans of soda were more sanitary than a cup of lemonade, they were more inclined to buy it. This young girl did this all summer. People loved this little girl. They recognized that she was an evolved entrepreneur and bought sodas from her.

Not everyone lives next to a post office. Not everyone has the opportunity to have a mom to help them with money. But if you find a niche that fits, try to fill that niche the best you can. There are banks that help people get started. There are government loans, like FHA, and USDA (see footnote on master's theses). Also, there are individuals and start-up lenders that may help you.

What Made Jane the Ultimate businessperson?

Without knowing it, she did everything successfully in starting and running a business, including the following:

Recognized a niche in the market

Saw an opportunity and acted on it

Found operating capital (Borrowed start-up money from her mom)

Kept a good accounting record of the money. She kept track of the cost of the product and recorded the expenses and sales.

Kept and managed a bank account

Paid back the loan for the start-up money

Found and used experienced help in starting a business (her mom)

Located in the perfect location

Had a fantastic customer base

Located a product at a great market price

Used FIFO (first in, first out)

Sold her product at a fair price

Had great quality control because the product was in a sealed can.

The product was kept cold in a cooler full of ice.

Marketed her product by placing several cans of her product on the table to advertise

Did basically anything and everything I could think of to have a successful business

When I had a chance, I explained this procedure to several young children that were starting a "Kool-Aid Stand." I have seen some of these stands change over to soda, and they have reported it was a success.

The Business Plan

Writing a business plan is probably the most important thing you do. I won't explain how to write a business plan here. If you don't know how to write one, get help. Find someone like a banker, accountant, businessman, business teacher, or experienced person to help. There are great programs you can purchase that tell how.

I will explain some things, that you may need to be on the lookout for, in starting a business.

How Do You Get Started? What Do You Do? Who Do You See?

One day, a friend and I were talking about business. She was thinking about starting her own hair salon. She asked me what I think are the smartest questions anyone could have asked: "How do you get started? What do you do? Who do you see?" Below are a few details I told her she may need for her hair salon, but this information will also work for many other businesses.

Government

On your computer, go to the Department of Commerce and register your business name.

Depending on which town you are in, get a business license.

Get a Tax ID.

Decide on a location and see if it is zoned for your business.

Get a sales tax number.

Get possible health department approval.

Get possible health department permits, like food handlers permit.

Owners

Who are the owners?

Whose name is on the lease and pays the rent?

Who owns the equipment, i.e., chairs, mirrors, table, driers, guest chairs, water heater, refrigerator, sinks, lights, curtains, rugs, mats, pictures, etc.?

Is there a CAM (common area maintenance)?

Who collects the rent for the chairs in hair salons?

Can you buy the building? Can you get a "right of first refusal"?

Whose name is on . . . and who pays the bills, light, gas, utilities, etc.

Do you have at least six months of start-up money set aside until your business gets going?

Do you personally have enough money to live for six months before you might make a profit?

Do you have a good accountant?

Do you have an exit plan in case you fail or in case you succeed and sell the business?

Is there a parking area?

Insurance

Do you have an insurance policy?

Whose name is on the policy?

Who gets sued if you color someone's hair yellow?

Who gets sued if you cut someone?

Who gets sued if someone slips on the floor?

What if you start a fire? Are the building and your equipment covered?

What if someone else starts the fire and your equipment is burned?

Do other beauticians have to have their own insurance?

Is there going to be a sign? Do you own it or rent it?

What happens if a window gets broken? Does your insurance cover it? Most renters have to pay for a broken window if it is broken from the inside, and the building owner pays for it if it is broken from the outside.

Daily Operations

How do you expect to make a profit?

Do you get a wage for being a manager?

Who collects the money from each customer?

Who collects the sales tax?

Who pays the sales taxes?

Whose name is on the federal tax forms?

How is the money collected?

What if all your partners quit? Are you stuck on the tax?

Do you have to show ALL the money on your income tax return?

Who is your competition?

What if you cannot work? Do you still have to pay for your help?

Don't forget to pay yourself.

With whom do you split the profits?

Do you have a good accountant?

Employees

How many are you going to have?

How many do you need to make a profit?

Do they have to have their own equipment?

Do they have to do their own cleaning around their chair?

Who cleans the sinks?

Who cleans the bathroom?

Who cleans the window?

Who mops the floor?

Who dusts the lights?

Who has a key to the store?

Who sets the schedule?

Who makes the appointment?

Is there a receptionist?

Do you take walk-ins?

Who assigns the customer to the beautician?

How do you fire a beautician?

What if they don't pay you on time?

What if they get tips? Do you get a share?

What if they lie?

Exit Strategy

(This is probably the most important thing to get right.)

Will your investors or partners buy you out?

If you quit, do your employees have a contract that says they get paid anyway?

Will they sue you for quitting?

Who will take charge if you get sick or want a vacation?

What if nothing goes well and you want to stop the business?

Are you still on the hook for the lease of the building?

Do you still have to pay employees?

Do you still have to pay back the loan for start-up, if any?

Do you still have to pay for equipment?

Do you still have to pay for supplies?

Will your partners or investors sue you?

If the store closes, will the bills keep coming, i.e., will there still be a bill for heating and electric so that the water pipes don't freeze or break?

And most importantly of all, what if you are a great success? Then what?

Perseverance

"Major Key to a Life of Success"

A definition of perseverance is "continued effort to do or achieve something despite difficulties, failure, or opposition; the action or condition or an instance of persevering: steadfastness" (from the Internet).

My eighth-grade schoolteacher started each day with a story or example of the word "perseverance." I think he was trying to instill in us the importance of never giving up. I never thought much about it, but looking back, he had a big impact on my brain because I have tried to persevere over and over in my life.

One summer, a federal dam failed just above my hometown. It completely devastated several towns. The loss of homes and businesses hurt the insurance business where I was working. It hurt the business so badly that I was out of work for a while. I had to find other work. A friend of mine helped me get a job at a lumber company. One of the major parts of the lumber company was selling and building pre-built homes in one location and moving them to the homeowners' prepared site, then finishing the project there. These homes were sold by dealers. As I mentioned, I had worked for my father in the insurance and real estate business. I thought being a dealer for these pre-built homes would work well with his existing business. I worked at the lumber company for a while and learned about the pre-built home business. I decided I wanted to be a dealer. I did my research for the town where I lived and found that this would be a good place for a dealer. I gave all my research to the field representative that came to the lumber company where I was working. He was very impressed and said he would present it to the pre-built home building business and determine if I could be a representative for them. I did not hear from him for several weeks, and he did not ever come back to the lumber yard again. So one day, I went to the pre-built home business office. I told them who I was and what research I had done. They said that they had never heard of me, but they knew about my research. They said that this field representative had used my research as his own and tried to get the dealership for himself. They did not like him much and said he was not very good as a fieldman. They had fired him and did not give him the dealership. After all was said and done, I got the dealership and went back to work in my father's business. The object here is that I was persistent in following up on the dealership.

Also, with regard to the dealership, I had no clue how to build a home. I had never built one before. But I knew other people had. I just needed to do some research on it.

My job working for the lumber company gave me great experience and education. While working there, I was taught how to read blueprints and determine how much cement, lumber, carpeting, etc. were needed to build each home. That experience was a major help in selling and building homes. I also visited the plant and found out what I needed to do before the completed unit was delivered to the location.

There were many things that had to be done, and most of them had to be done in order so that the next thing could be done. For example, the site had to have a building permit, and the foundation location had to be staked out. The water and sewer have to be staked out, and the depth of the hole for the foundation or basement had to be determined and dug. I had a good friend and an insurance client who owned and operated a back-hoe. He had experience in preparing sites for building. He was a big help, and I hired him over and over again. I also had friends and business acquaintances who worked in cement, electricity, plumbing, and framing. I chose people I knew and trusted as I built my business. This also helped many of my friends grow their businesses. After I built the first home, I felt very confident that I could build others, which I did. Once, I even built a six-unit apartment house. Persistence paid off.

My Motto Is . . .
"Go until I am told no, then go around that and try some more."

I started a business importing a drink from Hawaii to Utah. It is called Hawaiian Sun Juice. I was somewhat successful, and by working with a distributor and major grocery stores, I had the product in over a hundred stores. But the stores were not placing the product in the most effective spot. It was not selling very well. I decided to become my own distributor and discontinued my association with the stores and the distributor.

The product came from Hawaii in a full container that held twenty-one pallets, with one hundred cases on each pallet, with twenty-four cans per case. A container load held 50,400 cans. Only big outlets could handle that much product at a time. I set my sights on one of the biggest: Walmart. Cold calling is one thing, but for me, I thought, "You just don't walk into the biggest brick and motor store and ask, 'Do you want to buy my product?'" But that is exactly what I did. I made an appointment with one of the district managers and took in some samples. He said he was very busy, and I could have ten minutes. After exactly six minutes, he said, "Stop, I want it."

I think one reason he had worked his way up to district manager was that he knew how to make a decision. A few weeks later, other store managers came on board.

At that point, I started working with the main buyer in the home office. Things went well, but they were not sure if it would sell. I made them an offer. If they would let me put a single pallet containing one hundred cases of the product, in one of their stores; if it did not sell, I would buy the leftover product back at retail so there was no way they would lose money on the deal. 35 For some reason, the buyer did not understand exactly what we were trying to do, or he did not respect the district managers, or he just did not want to be bothered and did not want to do it. He and I did not get along very well. He even hung up on me on the phone. I asked my friend and CEO of the juice company to call him and see if he could explain what I was trying to do. The buyer also hung up on the CEO from Hawaii. He just refused to let us do the test of the product even though the stores wanted the product. There seemed to be no way to get past this man. I guess my motto of "Go until I am told no" was in place. But I had not been told no. I had been told yes by store managers. I decided to go over this man's head. I went to the internet. I found the person who was the head of this company. I wrote an actual paper letter to one of the CEOs, explaining the situation and how rude the employee had been to us. A short time later, an executive called me, and after explaining everything to him, he said he would have the buyer call me and set it up. Long story short, I got the product to many of the stores.

Sometimes, continue to "go" even if you are told no.

Networking

I want to stop here and insert a bit of information on "networking." I have lived in many towns. Along the way, I have met some fantastic friends—friends that I know would help me if and when I needed them. I have mentioned to my family that I have a friend in a couple of hundred miles in any direction. And there have been times when I have had to call on my friends for help. There have been times when my friends have asked me for help, and I have been able to serve them. One example: When my son was traveling, from visiting me to returning to his home about 120 miles away, he called me on his way and said that the pickup he was driving had just broken down. It just so happened that the pickup had broken down on the freeway just in front of one of my friend's homes. I called my friend. I asked him to look out his window and see if he could see my son's vehicle. He could. My son could not believe that a friend of mine showed up to help in a matter of minutes of him calling me. As it happened, my friend owned a trucking company and had a big shop at his home. He towed my son's pickup to his house and, within a short time, had him back on the road again. It is good to have a "network" of friends that can help you when you need them. It is also good to be a friend so that when your friend needs something, you can be there for them.

Learning from Your Network

I worked as a schoolteacher as my main occupation. I loved being a schoolteacher. I loved the kids I taught, and I loved the subject of business. But, as most teachers have to do, I had other jobs that I did to supplement my income. I tried several ways to supplement my income, including teaching night school, working as a clerk in a lumber store, being a host in some restaurants,

Along the way, I felt like we needed more retirement setup. I tried to build a convenience store several times but did not get it done. I also have always felt that we needed equity in something for the future. A friend of mine built an Arctic Circle restaurant in a small town. I did not think a major chain restaurant would do well in a small town, but I was wrong. It was a great success. I looked around and decided that the town in which I was living was about the same size as the one my friend lived in. In fact, we had more people and a higher traffic count in the area I wanted to build the restaurant. I checked into every aspect of building an Arctic Circle restaurant. I even invited the people from Arctic Circle to come to my town and check it out. They thought it was a very good idea. Now, I only had one problem: I did not have any money. I found a couple of good locations. Since I was new to this town, I asked friends who they thought was the richest man in town. They gave me some names. One just so happened to be the owner of one of the properties I liked. I called the owner and ask him if he would talk to me about selling the ground. He said he would. Our meeting went well, and at the end of my explanation, I told him I did not have enough money to do what I wanted to do. I asked if he "would like to back me" instead of just selling me the ground. His exact words were, "Sure, why not?" I can tell one reason why this man was rich. It was because he was able to make quick decisions.

I originally wanted to just borrow the start-up money from him and offered him 12 percent interest plus 4 percent of the profits. I researched several loans, and we finally settled on an SBA loan from a local bank. However, SBA needed more money down. My backer did not want to put that much money into the project. However, he had two friends who wanted to get in on this, so the four of us became partners.

Because the first three partners put in the money and I put in the time and experience in starting a new business, we settled on a 33 percent, 33 percent, 16.5 percent, 16.5 percent split ownership in the business. I ended up with only a 16.5 percent share of the business. This amount was not what I envisioned as an owner when I started this business, but when you don't have any money, you play by the "Golden Rule." He who has the gold makes the rules. From then on, everything went well. You learn something with every experience. This was a completely new experience for me. I was dealing with partners, employees, inventory, customers, bills, income, ordering the product, and many more things that were new to me. One of the things I did not plan for was my monthly salary. I thought I would make my money by being a bigger owner of the business. Now, I was a part-owner, but only with my 16.5 percent ownership, I was also an employee. However, I was not getting a salary for working on a daily basis. I guess this was one of those times when I was way better at starting a business than running it. Because I needed a steady income coming in every month, a decision was made to sell my share of the business back to the partners and get out of the restaurant business. So I sold my part of the business and went back into teaching. I felt it was a great experience, and I made a good profit from putting it together.

Ethics

Having good ethics may be the most important point I make in this book. Ethics is one of the most important tools a businessman or woman can have in their business toolbox. Unfortunately, some people do not subscribe to the reasoning.

Taken from the Internet, some definitions of ethics are the following:

"Moral principles that govern a person's behavior or the conducting of an activity"

"Ethics refers to well-founded standards of right and wrong that prescribe what humans ought to do, usually in terms of rights, obligations, benefits to society, fairness, or specific virtues."

"The term ethics may refer to the philosophical study of the concepts of moral right and wrong and moral good and bad, to any philosophical theory of what is morally right and wrong or morally good and bad, and to any system or code of moral rules, principles, or values."

I would like to say that I don't care how good of a businessman or woman you are, you will never succeed if you don't have good ethics, but that is not true. Unfortunately, a lot of people have very good success in business by having no ethics at all. And, some people, in a position of power, manipulate and take advantage of others.

I have never liked working with those types of people, and I know a lot of people who will not work with them either. I have passed on a lot of business opportunities because I felt they were a bit shady or not up to the standards, which I have set for myself.

I have mentioned a few people who I believe did not have very good ethics. There were the people who stole my pigs, the person who took all my information and tried to make it his own in the home building business, and the CEO that hung up on me.

Another example of what I consider poor ethics happened while we were building the Arctic Circle. I mentioned that I had looked at a couple of good locations for the Arctic Circle.

Before getting the agreement with the owner of the property on which we were going to build, I had asked another land owner if he want to back me. He had turned me down. I found out later that he had called the AC headquarters and was complaining to them that they should be sending him all the information and not me because it was his land and money we were using.

What he was trying to do was take all my information and cut me out of everything. He even tried to hire a friend of mine as a manager. I did not want to confront him about this, but I did visit him again. I wanted to give him a chance to redeem himself. When I asked him again if he wanted to back me, he said he did not have time and was not interested. Again, I am completely baffled how someone could even try to do something like that. Anyway, we did build the restaurant. We had the biggest grand opening Arctic Circle had ever had up until that time. It was a success.

Recordkeeping/Accounting

I cannot emphasize the importance of good recordkeeping.

There are several ways to keep records or notes. First, get a good notebook or pad and keep it with you to keep current notes. Another way is to create files on your computer for each segment of your business. For example, keep one file for contacts; different businesses with which you deal; different departments such as accounts, accounts receivable, and payable, invoices; purchase orders; banking; home office; salespeople; wife; husband; kids; and many more. I have a general file on business, and within that file are subfiles for many of the things mentioned.

Some of the things you need to record are dates, times, names, organizations, departments, and contents. Again, ALWAYS RECORD A DATE.

You get the idea. Just get used to doing this as it is happening or as soon as possible after the conversation takes place. You will never regret this. Things can come back to bite you. Even the poorest notes can save your bacon in a court of law or put you in the first place when it comes to proving you contacted that business or person before someone else.

I have gone back in files that are very old and thought I would never need that information again, but I did.

Money, Money, Money

Everything you do needs money and more money. As I mentioned above, you need start-up money for everything including permits, equipment, staffing, product, and maybe a building. But you also need money to live on while your business is getting started, etc.

The best kind of money is OPM. OPM stands for "other people's money."

OPM means you do not use your money but get money from other places like banks, businesses, or individuals. It does not mean it's free. You usually have to pay interest. It is a cost of doing business. However, it does have several advantages.

It is not just your money. It also puts OPM at risk. You share the risk.

A lot of people like to invest. It can be a good investment for them, usually because the interest rate you pay for the use of this money is higher than they can get in a savings account.

It can sometimes also be a tax right-off.

OPM is usually secured very well, like with property.

It can be faster than going through a bank.

Usually, OPM does not require as much paperwork and personal information.

I have used OPM many times. I have had people willing to carry a contract on several homes I have purchased. If they are in a position to do it, they like it because it means a quick sale for them, and they make interest.

Ask for a Discount
(This will save you a lot of money.)

Other people's money (OPM) can be extremely helpful if your business goes well and you need to expand, advertise, change locations, or buy more products.

Also, as part of OPM, always ask for a discount. I will repeat this. Always, always, always, ask for a discount on everything. I have asked for and received a discount on everything—from cars to houses and from products to rent. Because I had used him once before, I even got a discount on my wife's breast implants from a plastic surgeon. The list goes on and on. Some places are set up to give a discount, like to military or senior citizens. Other places will do it if you ask. You just need to ask.

What? Wait? What?

Once when I was in a department store, I saw some candy that I liked. On the outside of the box, it advertised that there was a coupon on the inside the box for a free box of candy when you bought this one. So I took it up to the cashier, paid for it, and then opened it while I was still at the counter. I took out the coupon and asked the cashier if I could use it for the free box. She said yes. The store was not busy, so I offered her a piece of candy, and I went back and got another box of candy.

I am going to stop right here and ask you to think about what I just wrote. Wait for it. Can you see anything unusual about this? If not, you are definitely not an entrepreneur.

Okay, here is the obvious answer. If one box gives me a coupon, I can get a second coupon in the next box and get a free box with another coupon for a free box, and another coupon and another free box, and so on, and so on. I emptied out the complete shelf of candy. I ended up with about thirty boxes of candy and only paid for the first box. I am not sure the genius advertising person who came up with this idea really had that in mind when they put it in the box. Maybe if they had put on the coupon something like, "One per customer" or "Buy one, get one free," it would have made them some extra sales. I am pretty sure that by using my idea, the cashier made out like a bandit the next day when they refilled the shelves.

Teach Your Children to Spend Money

Here is a tip on how to help your children learn how to spend money. Yes, I said spend money, not save money. Spending and saving go hand-in-hand.

1. The first 10 percent: Teach your children that if they earn a dollar, divide it into four parts. The first section is worth 10 percent. This 10 percent is for charity. Teach them to give it away to a church, a nonprofit origination, a charity, or just someone who needs it. As an example, a few days before Thanksgiving, my parents used to take an envelope and put enough cash in it to purchase everything needed for a Thanksgiving dinner. They would take four or five of them to the grocery store, give one envelope to a different cashier, and tell them what it was and give it to someone who they knew always came through their station and needed it. It is important that children learn to be charitable.

2. The next 30 percent: 30 percent should be put into what I call "permanent savings." This amount of money is not to be spent at that time. It is savings—maybe to be used later in life for a car or college. Just put it in a bank and forget about it. Do not spend it.

3. The second 30 percent: This 30 percent is what I call "spending savings." This amount of money is saved for a purpose. For example, one of your kids may want to buy a new camera or skateboard. This is the money they save up and use for the item.

4. The last 30 percent: The last 30 percent is what I call "walking around money" or "pocket money." Kids need to have money to spend. Start early. Even little kids need to know that if they pick up their toys and mom or dad pays them with real money, this money can be used to buy real things. Children in middle school and high school, especially, need to have "spending money." Sometimes, friends will invite them to go to the mall

or a movie, and they need money to buy a soda or treat. If they learn to spend it wisely, they will learn to save it.

Luck Is When Opportunity Meets the Prepared

One of the things that have happened to me over the years is that I often wake up in the middle of the night, usually around about two or three in the morning. Sometimes, my brain is often working overtime, and I cannot go back to sleep. I used to fight this. I would try to go back to sleep or just get up and watch television for a while. Now I accept it and even relish it. I get up and start writing down things I am thinking about. Usually, once I do this, I can go back to sleep. Many times it would be the solution to a problem I have been working on in the daytime. I have used this technique many times. Part of this book was written in the middle of the night. I think that this is part of my entrepreneurial brain kicking in.

> "Your mind will answer most questions if you
> learn to relax and wait for the answer."
> —William S. Burroughs

And what if it doesn't? Things sometimes don't go your way or may go your way but not in your time frame. Relax. What is the worst thing that can happen? Over my lifetime, I have had a lot of money, and I have been very low on funds. I have had great success and have failed many times. That is the world of an entrepreneur. Time will usually fix most things. It is like a roller-coaster ride. It has its ups and its downs. I just hope you enjoy the ride.

In Conclusion

Is this everything you need to know to start a business? No, not even close. However, if you research every aspect of starting and running a business, I think you will never open one. Then you are not an entrepreneur. But if you know enough to get started, you will open one and then figure out how to make it a success. Then, you are a true entrepreneur.

It is all right to learn from people who have done things you want to do. I am very grateful to the many people who have helped me throughout my life. I hope the information contained in this book will help you. I hope it gives you some things to watch for as you start your business. And I hope this information keeps you from being surprised as you work to get your business going.

Good luck. Now, go to work.

Autobiography
of
Roger M. Rowan

Who you are and what you do can help determine if you succeed?

One of the things that have been a constant with me throughout my life is my faith in the Lord and my testimony of my church. Over the years, I have done things that I really don't think I could have done without the help of someone or something bigger than I am.

An example of this was when I bought my current home.

In 2013, I moved back to Logan, Utah, from Boise, Idaho. I had retired from school teaching and had moved to Boise to be near some of my grandchildren. About a year later, they moved back to Utah, so I did too. I had sold my home, lawn mower, rake, and everything else I needed to be a homeowner. I decided I did not want to own a home but just rent.

After a few years, I decided I wanted to buy a home again and started looking. I like the idea of the fifty-five and older subdivisions that have been growing in my area because the HOA provided the service of lawn care and snow removal. I started looking a couple of years ago. I found a few homes I liked, but I could not find the exact one I wanted. My loan was for the rural area only. I was told by my lending company that the town of Hyde Park did not qualify, so I did not look here. Later, a builder said the north part of Hyde Park did qualify.

I was sitting in my recliner one Sunday afternoon, in my apartment, when I heard a voice say to me, "Get up out of this recliner right now and go to Hyde Park." I was surprised because I wasn't even thinking about a house or moving at that time. I don't mean that the voice was out loud. If someone else had been in my living room, I don't think they would have heard it. But I heard it as loud as if there had been someone else in my living room. I decided to follow that guidance. I got up and jumped in my car and headed North. I was not even sure where to turn to go to Hyde Park. When I go to the Maverik store at Hyde Park, I heard the same voice say, "Turn right here." I did. When I got up to the post office, the voice again said, "Turn right here. I did. I went about five hundred yards, and there was the fifty-five and older subdivision I am in now. I saw people moving out of the first house I came to. I stopped and talked to them, but they said they were going to rent it instead of selling it. I could not see any for sale signs, so I left and came back the next day. I saw a man working on his truck in his driveway. I stopped and introduced myself to him and asked if he knew anyone in the area who was thinking of moving. He pointed to the house a couple of doors down and said they were selling. I went over there. I found the doors open but no one around. The house was mostly empty. I went around back, and there was the daughter of the man that was selling it. I said, "I heard you were selling this home, is that right?"

She said, "Yes," and I said, "Okay, I want to buy it."

She looked at me like I was a little crazy and asked if I have been inside. I said no but that I have been inside of several other homes like this, and although I don't know their color scheme, I did know the floor plan. She said, "Well, come in."

Within a few weeks, I had bought the home and moved in. The man from whom I bought the home was eighty-five years old. His wife had died just a short time ago. A week later, he went to visit another piece of property he owned in a mountain area, got stuck in the snow, tried to walk home, and died of either a heart attack or froze to death.

I felt I was very lucky to have purchased this home when I did. What if I had not listened to the voice that told me to get up off my chair. Some people may say that that was just a coincidence or luck, or my mind just came up with this thought. Some people might even say it was the "Akashic records." I truly believe it was the Holy Spirit of God.

If you are an entrepreneur, the following statement will be redundant to you, but *never give up*. I was also prepared and had done my homework in searching for a home. I felt very blessed and lucky. Luck is when opportunity meets the prepared.

A Pot of Gold at the End of a Rainbow

A couple of interesting things came out of starting and owning the Arctic Circle restaurant.

One, I was able to use the information I gathered in obtaining a loan from the government for my thesis, and I finish my master's degree.

The following is the title of my master's thesis:

A report submitted in partial fulfillment of the requirements for the degree of Masters of Social Science Interdepartmental Program in Public Administration. "A Description and Analysis of Gaining a Small Business Loan from a Public Agency United States Department of Agriculture (Farmers Home Administration) Utah State University, Logan Utah 1992 by Roger M. Rowan

And two, I was still a schoolteacher at the time, and because I was able to offer about twenty-five high school kids a job working for the Arctic Circle, I won the Utah Young Entrepreneur of the Year" from the state of Utah Education Department.

www.ingramcontent.com/pod-product-compliance
Lightning Source LLC
Chambersburg PA
CBHW021513210526
45463CB00002B/1003